The Second World War was a 'total war' in which civilians were targeted, as well as those armed to fight. Everyone in Britain, babies included, was issued with a gas mask to wear in case of poisoned gas attack. Construction of air raid shelters began. Night-time blackout was ordered in cities from 1 September, the day on which mass evacuation also started. In three days, around 1.5 million people – many of them children – had been transported to rural areas. Two million others had already moved to the country-side, or sought safety overseas.

And then – apart from a few stray bombs – nothing much happened. National morale dipped in this 'Phoney War' period and fell further in April 1940 when, stunned by the German advance into Denmark, Norway, the Low Countries and France, Chamberlain resigned. King George VI sent for Winston Churchill and asked him to form a new government.

Churchill rallied the nation during the evacuation of Dunkirk and throughout the Battle of Britain. For a German inva-sion to succeed, the Luftwaffe had first to destroy the Royal Air Force. But when the RAF's heroic defence of Britain's skies wrecked Hitler's plans, the Germans switched their attack to British cities.

LEFT: Gas masks, issued to all, were to be carried 'at all times'. These young evacuees on the south coast have taken the message seriously.

MAIN PICTURE: Road casualties rose alarmingly during the blackout in the first weeks of war, so government posters urged caution.

UNTIL YOUR EYES GET USED TO THE DARKNESS, TAKE IT EASY

OOK OUT IN THE BLACKOUT

MORNING COFFEE

CAFE OPEN

3

LONDON BURNING

ABOVE: October 1940, Balham High Road: a bomb landed 23 metres (25 yards) in front of this bus, which began 'prancing about like a horse' (the driver's words), then fell into the crater.

With the wailing of sirens on Saturday 7 September 1940, the Blitz began. It was a hot summer afternoon around 5.00 pm. A droning hum first signalled the approach of hundreds of enemy aircraft. It grew to a deafening roar. Then came the thud and air-rending crash of exploding bombs. People rushed pell-mell for shelter.

The first bombs fell on Woolwich Arsenal, then on the London docks. Soon the tightly packed houses of the East End were under attack. A second wave followed later that evening and into the early hours. By the morning, 430 East Enders lay dead in their ravaged streets and gardens.

The docks blazed. 'Everything was alight including the warehouses and everything inside them was burning, the fumes choked you.' Flames and billowing acrid smoke flared up from the furnace of burning rum, sugar, paint, rubber and timber stored in warehouses beside the Thames. Only the heroic efforts of London's firemen saved the city as they battled non-stop for two days against searing heat and poisonous fumes.

The Blitz was meant to open the way for the Nazi invasion of Britain. But Hitler lost the Battle of London because he could not break its people's spirit. For 57 consecutive nights, Londoners endured saturation bombing as thousands of tons of incendiaries and explosives cascaded from the sky. Familiar landmarks vanished; others, like the Houses of Parliament and Buckingham Palace, suffered damage. Over 12,000 people were killed; 20,000 were badly injured. Through it all, Londoners kept going. They got up each morning and went to work. There were no stoppages or strikes during the Blitz and absenteeism was minimal. Work was a comforting routine. Shared hardship and loss created tremendous solidarity allied with a determination to 'deserve victory'. Londoners had not buckled. Britain would not give in.

ABOVE: King George VI and Queen Elizabeth chat to a rescue worker. The royal family remained in London despite the bombing.

BRITAIN IN
THE BLITZ

THE FIRST BOMBS FALL

In 1940, from July to December, death rained from the skies onto British cities. In six months, a sustained bombing campaign killed more civilians – ordinary men, women and children – than died on active service. Intended to crush the fight out of Britain, instead it inspired a new spirit – the spirit of the Blitz.

'Blitz' was short for blitzkrieg, the 'lightning war' tactic devastatingly employed by German forces in Poland (1939), and in Belgium, the Netherlands and France (1940). Its basic elements were surprise, speed and overwhelming firepower: motorized artillery, tanks and aircraft.

Britain knew what to expect. It had seen Adolf Hitler's Nazi Party rise to power in Germany and watched Luftwaffe bombers aid armoured panzer divisions to overrun much of Europe. Preparations for possible air bombardment of Britain were under way well before Prime Minister Neville Chamberlain declared Britain to be at war on 3 September 1939, following Germany's invasion of Poland.

BELOW: A child waits in June 1940 for a train to take her from the London bomb zone. Of thousands evacuated, many soon returned.

RIGHT: The day war broke out: 3 September 1939. Newspapers declared what many had been anticipating for months.

ABOVE: Preparations for bombing had begun before the war. Glass-fronted premises such as this café were sandbagged against blast and shrapnel.

LEFT: Word spread quickly when bargains were to be had, of food, clothing or bomb-damaged goods. Shoppers became used to shortages and queues.

RIGHT: A Home Guard volunteer gives rifle instruction to a member of the Women's Home Defence unit. Fear of imminent invasion was real in the early months of war.

BELOW: Over the target. On 7 September 1940, a German Heinkel 111 aims its bombs on London. Below, the River Thames winds through the East End and docklands.

THE HOME GUARD

One of the Churchill government's first acts had been to form the Local Defence Volunteers, soon to be renamed the Home Guard. Men in their thousands rushed to join, some in their 70s and 80s! They were responsible for seeking out enemy parachutists as part of their job of home defence. But the Home Guard was also charged with the last-ditch defence of London, which Hitler saw as his principal target. Anti-tank lines were prepared with trenches, road blocks, barriers and pillboxes, some of which were disguised as petrol stations or tea stalls!

BELOW: Tea and sympathy for survivors: a life saved, but a home lost. Many never forgot the smells of smoke, charred timbers, escaping gas, and the chemical stench of high explosive.

CITY STRIKES

Only one house in ten escaped damage in central London, but by October 1940 the Luftwaffe had switched to smaller targets, striking Coventry and Birmingham seven times that month.

The night of 14 November proved to be critical. Churchill had been warned of a huge raid planned, but the precise target was not at first known. Cities were put on defensive alert, but none could have withstood the fury unleashed on the sleeping city of Coventry, as 400 bombers aimed for its heart. By 3.30 am the city was ablaze. Daybreak dawned on the city's smoking ruins: the medieval cathedral all but destroyed, its spire alone towering over collapsed walls.

During the winter of 1940–41, raiders bombed other vital industrial centres and ports: Bristol, Liverpool, Southampton, Manchester, Sheffield, Swansea, Glasgow, Plymouth and Hull. Water froze in the firefighters' hoses during the Bristol raid of 3–4 January 1941. A Women's Voluntary Service (WVS) worker recalled, 'The firemen put their cups of tea down and they froze. The tea froze. The hose froze. We had a choice of being frozen, burned, blown up or drowned in tea.'

Luftwaffe tactics were to drop incendiaries on city centres, often on Sunday nights when most workers were at home. Southampton, Sheffield and

ABOVE: Bombing bared the ruins of private lives as crumbled buildings exposed skeletons of former homes.

Manchester were bombed in December, and Coventry again in April 1941. An estimated 800 planes attacked Merseyside on successive nights between 1 and 7 May 1941. Although attacks eased around the end of the month, raids continued to be targeted on east coast cities such as Hull.

The bombers later found new prey: heritage sites. The so-called Baedeker raids, named after the famous guidebooks supposedly used by German pilots, pinpointed ancient towns such as Canterbury, York, Bath and Norwich. Coastal towns, including Dover and Eastbourne, were battered by 'tip and run' raiders, while enemy planes, singly or in small formations, appeared over the coast from Cornwall to Aberdeen. Causing little significant damage, the raids proved talking points for local citizens who grew accustomed to wailing air raid sirens disrupting daily life. People were advised to carry on after the first sirens sounded and wait for the klaxon blasts from rooftop observers that signalled enemy aircraft were in sight.

ABOVE: Streets became temporary stores or markets for salvaged furniture. People were brought together by the shared horrors and discomforts of war from the air.

MAIN PICTURE: Coventry Cathedral ruins. More than 500 people died on 14 November 1940 when enemy aircraft bombed the city.

INSET: In the aftermath of a raid, members of the WVS (Women's Voluntary Service) serve reviving cups of tea to a thirsty rescue squad.

CHINS UP

The people of Britain now faced nightly air attack – even night-long bombardment, as in Sheffield on 12 December 1940, when the raid lasted nine hours. Before the war, people had queried the effects of such bombing on morale. Would it cause apathy, panic, even riots?

By and large, such fears were groundless. What happened? People just carried on. Faced with driving her canteen van through blacked-out, rubble-strewn streets, one WVS worker took her son along. Lying on the bonnet, he called out directions as she nosed slowly forward down a road criss-crossed by fire hoses and tangled cables. If the way was completely blocked, rescuers walked – carrying first aid equipment, shovels, tea – whatever was needed.

Damage was severe: in Portsmouth, 60,000 of the city's 70,000 homes were affected. After the 1941 'May week' raids, 40,000 people in Liverpool were left homeless. Within a week, all had been billeted within the city, moved to rest centres or to other towns and villages. Repairing buildings and resettling families became a major headache, but somehow people coped. An observer in Liverpool was startled to see women cleaning their front steps and polishing any windows that had survived the night's blasts! 'To begin with we'd all been shocked by the raids and panicked. But after a few weeks you got used to it … I'd cycle to work every day, even though there might be …

ABOVE: People were glad to have meals cooked by neighbours who still had gas or electricity.

bombs falling … you were angry at all the destruction … You had to keep going, to keep up the fight against Hitler.'

People slept when and where they could. They ate food hot when gas and electricity were switched on; and cold when they were off. They went to work more or less on time and sent their children to school. It was assumed that 'normal life' would continue – and somehow it usually did. Swansea children in Sunday-best dresses and suits turned out on debris-choked streets to go to chapel. Shops opened in city centres, ignoring blown-out windows and stock scattered across the street. ARP (Air Raid Precautions) wardens patrolled their local area, checked blackout and organized rescue work.

Families saved whatever they could to help personalize temporary accommodation.

RIGHT: It was not all smiles. A little girl is comforted by a woman rescuer, while the faces around her tell their own story.

BELOW: The cash register may not work, and the shopfront has gone, but a customer is still a customer.

ABOVE: WVS workers demonstrate how to build an emergency brick oven.

People were eager to 'do their bit' for the war effort. For some, this meant joining the Fire Guard – a vital arm of home defence set up in summer 1941. Firewatching was a nightly duty for many men and women not enrolled in the Home Guard or Civil Defence. Their defensive weapons were sand and a stirrup pump. German incendiaries were only 30cm (1 foot) long. Dump a bucket of sand on them and the danger was over. Throwing water caused the bomb to fragment, spreading more fires, but the fine spray from a stirrup pump doused the device safely. Speed could prevent a small firebomb from burning down an entire factory.

In the front line of neighbourhood defence was the ARP warden who, when a bomb fell, ran to the local wardens' post. Details were telephoned to the control centre, which in turn alerted whatever emergency services (fire, ambulance, heavy rescue) could be spared. The priority was to rescue survivors and treat casualties. It was a well-practised routine: search and rescue, make safe damaged buildings, list casualties, move survivors to rest and emergency feeding centres. Then came repair: rehouse homeless families, salvage furniture and personal possessions, reconnect gas, electricity and water.

Britain could take it, but it also fought back. Searchlights, often operated by women of the ATS, probed the night sky for raiders. Barrage balloons and anti-aircraft (AA or 'ack-ack') guns tried to force enemy planes to fly too high for accurate bombing. To detect incoming bombers, Britain used somewhat primitive range-finders and echo-locators. But it also had a priceless asset – radar. Until the spring of 1941, RAF pilots were often 'blind' in the night sky, unable to find and shoot down enemy bombers. In December 1940 the 'kill rate' was one German bomber in 326; by March 1941, largely due to improved radar, this had risen to one in 63.

Women of the Auxiliary Territorial Service (or ATS) operated equipment such as height-finding devices, below, but did not fire the AA guns.

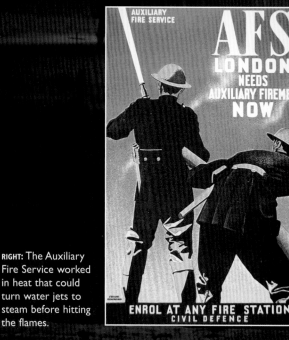

RIGHT: The Auxiliary Fire Service worked in heat that could turn water jets to steam before hitting the flames.

AUXILIARY FIRE SERVICE

AFS
LONDON
NEEDS
AUXILIARY FIREMEN
NOW

ENROL AT ANY FIRE STATION
CIVIL DEFENCE

ABOVE: Men and women from all walks of life prepared to face the threat of German troops.

ABOVE: A cigarette card shows how a stirrup pump, used promptly, could stop an incendiary bomb starting a serious fire.

Thousands of barrage balloons floated in the skies, each needing a crew of 10 men or 16 women to keep it aloft.

ABOVE: Leftovers saved for public 'pig bins' ensured that Britain's porkers had not too lean a time.

Fearful that shortages of food and materials might lower morale, the government hotted up its propaganda war, aiming to combat 'defeatism' and encourage thrift. Leaflets expounded the horrors of Nazism. Posters urged people to 'save fuel for battle', 'walk when you can', 'dig for victory', wage war on the 'squander bug'. Mrs Sew and Sew, needle in hand, beamed from the Make Do and Mend posters devised by the Board of Trade. Women were urged to attend sewing classes, and learn how to 'turn' collars or make coats from blankets and flour sacks.

Clothing was rationed from June 1941 and in March 1942 came the launch of Utility clothes, designed to use minimum material. Saving and salvage became national passions. Children toured the streets collecting waste paper, glass bottles, tins and silver paper for re-use. Some sang 'There'll always be a dustbin …'.

The Ministry of Food administered rationing through 1,300 regional offices. Each person was issued with a ration book of tear-out coupons to exchange in food shops. Healthy eating was encouraged in advertisements featuring Doctor 'guards your health' Carrot and Potato 'I'm an energy food' Pete. Since carrots were said to improve night-sight, people in blacked-out Britain ate them enthusiastically. The National Wheatmeal Loaf was less popular; it was coarse, husky and an unappetizing grey-brown.

Foreign fruits such as oranges and bananas vanished from greengrocers. People dug up lawns to grow their own vegetables; some kept chickens or rabbits. Dried egg from the USA could be eaten scrambled or used in cakes. Plaster models replaced fruit-filled wedding cakes with decorative icing. Charles Hill, the 'Radio Doctor', broadcast advice on healthy eating, and Lord Woolton, heading the Ministry of Food, gave his name to 'Woolton pie', made from carrots, parsnips, turnips and potatoes. People hung on to traditional pleasures somehow. War or no war, surveys by Mass Observation reported in 1943, 'the Sunday joint still appears on every table'. In some households, some weeks, the 'joint' was a kipper.

In spring 1941, the adult weekly food ration included: 3 pints of milk, 2oz (55g) of tea, 4oz (170g) of margarine or cooking fat, 2oz (55g) butter, 8oz (225g) jam or honey, 8oz (225g) sugar, 2oz (55g) cheese, 4oz (115g) bacon or ham, and a small piece of meat (equivalent to two small chops). As supplies from the USA increased, each person might also claim a tin of Spam and a packet of dried egg.

ABOVE: The weekly food ration, with the coupon book needed to buy it. Babies and children had 'extras' of milk, cod liver oil and orange juice.

LEFT: Sewing skills were put to work in parachute-making, too, as well as clothes alterations.

Go through your wardrobe

Make-do and Mend

ABOVE: A Board of Trade poster urging families to be creative with their well-worn clothes to make them last longer.

BELOW: Women without cosmetics and stockings found ways to improvise. Beetroot juice reddened lips, while legs could be 'painted' to give an illusion of silkiness.

BELOW: Children hoped their scrap would metamorphose into a Spitfire.

NO MORE LADDERS

We paint your stockings on your legs

ALL SHADES Per 3ᵈ a leg

When the sirens sounded their whining rise and fall, people headed for shelter. The government had issued 2.5 million Anderson shelters to households by the early days of the war. Made of corrugated steel and covered with soil, the Anderson was cramped and let in rainwater, but could withstand anything less than a direct hit. 'We had a very happy little atmosphere in our shelter' ... '[ours] had a little cooker, electric light' ... 'we had a little Pifco toaster which gave us the chance of doing a bit of toast and dripping if we felt peckish ...'. In 1941 the Home Secretary, Herbert Morrison, introduced an indoor shelter (the Morrison) for homes without gardens. It looked like a table, and indeed could be used as one.

Public shelters were unpopular, especially those looking like hastily constructed brick boxes with concrete roofs. Dark, cold and often stinking of urine, the badly built structures were liable to collapse under blast impact. London's Tilbury shelter, an underground railway goods yard, provided refuge for up to 16,000 people a night, but in squalid conditions. More attractive were Chislehurst Caves in Kent, and by October 1940, 15,000 residents had moved into this huge natural shelter.

London's tube stations also provided underground refuge from the bombing, although the government initially feared this would breed 'passivity' instead of resilience. From September 1940, however, thousands flooded to the stations, after buying a 1½d (1p) ticket, the cheapest fare. Over 150,000 Londoners slept nightly on the platforms, on escalators and in hammocks over the rails after the power was switched off.

After a while, people grew used to the sirens' wail and stayed in their homes for as long as possible before taking cover. They listened to the wireless, prepared evening meals, experimented with recipes for carrot jam, read the newspaper or tried to blot out the Blitz with diversions from dance music to dominoes. When the siren sent out its long, steady 'All clear' note, the raid was over.

ABOVE: A pint and a sing-song helped to keep up spirits.

BELOW: 'Firebomb Fritz' – another name for incendiary bombs from the ever-busy Ministry of Information.

Beat 'FIREBOMB FRITZ'

BRITAIN SHALL NOT BURN

BRITAIN'S FIRE GUARD IS BRITAIN'S DEFENCE

ABOVE: People dug a pit to enclose their Anderson shelter, taking to it only when the siren sounded.

RIGHT: A hammock slung between rails in the Underground makes a safe bed for a pair of young Londoners.

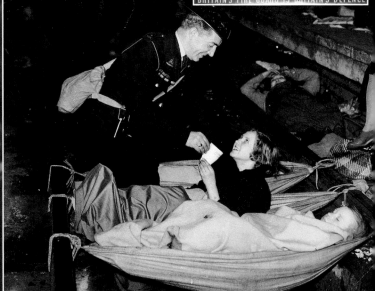

MAIN PICTURE: Sleeping in the Underground became a nightly routine for thousands of Londoners.

RUG-MAKING FOR BLACK-OUT NIGHTS

WOMAN'S FRIEND

2d

SPECIAL DESIGNS *inside*

ABOVE: Women's magazines advised on everything from babycare to blackout pastimes.

ABOVE: People could sleep in the wire 'cage' of the Morrison shelter, protected by a steel top.

TOP: If a house was hit, the Morrison might buckle, but remained intact beneath the debris.

'More open than usual' was a sign displayed, with rueful humour, outside many bomb-devastated shops that claimed to be 'shattered not shut-tered'. With a mixture of fear and bravado, people endured the nightly raids. They suffered deprivation, disruption, destruction, disorientation and loss. And they rose to the challenge. Churchill's rasping defiance bolstered their own conviction that defeat was impossible. 'We will never surrender.' Victory would come.

Humour was a powerful weapon in raising morale. So was popular music, either cheery or sentimental. Cinemas, dance halls and pubs opened as usual, though some people preferred to steer clear of crowds.

ABOVE: Families did their best to celebrate Christmas in 1940, though the news was grim. Liverpool and Manchester were hit by heavy raids at that time.

ABOVE: Blitz humour helped raise a smile on dark, cold mornings as people went to work on yet another 'morning after' a raid.

ABOVE: People took every opportunity to relax and enjoy themselves. Open-air dancing was fun even in the shadow of a wallowing barrage balloon.

The cinema provided escape for a couple of hours in companionable darkness. Government propaganda films and newsreels, sometimes fatuously optimistic, were balanced by a continuous flow of American feature films and cartoons. Magazines provided both graphic war pictures and escapism, attracting millions of readers to *Picture Post, Woman, Illustrated, John Bull* and *Picturegoers' Film Weekly*.

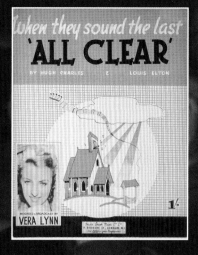

ABOVE: Some of the songs recorded by 'Forces' Sweetheart' Vera Lynn have become enduringly associated with the 'spirit of the Blitz'.

People found company and a friendly word in clubs and canteens. To raise flagging spirits, the BBC pumped out dance band music and comedies such as Tommy Handley's *ITMA*, with Mrs Mopp's much-repeated catchphrase, 'Can I do you now, sir?' Two popular radio programmes, *Workers' Playtime* and *Music While You Work*, were introduced to lift spirits on the factory floor and boost production.

Other odd sights served to raise sagging spirits: vegetables growing in the Tower of London's moat; pigs in the drained swimming bath at the Ladies' Carlton Club in London.

Shoppers snapped up bomb-damaged goods at bargain prices – 'hard wearing mattress beds, ideal for shelters, for only 25 shillings' (£1.25). At Westminster, those emerging from a shelter next to the Woodstock Snack Bar could buy, from 6.00 am, an 'air raid breakfast' for 1s 8d (8p).

In 1941 the United States entered the war, after the Japanese attack on Pearl Harbor. The war tide began to turn. Now Germany endured bombing by the Allies; the RAF by night and US Army Air Force by day. The first – and worst – stage of Britain's Blitz was over. Yet further unwelcome surprises in the German armoury were unleashed in 1944, however, when the south of England was hit by V-1 flying bombs and – the Nazis' ultimate weapon – the supersonic V-2 rocket.

BELOW: Radio's most popular comedy show of the war: *ITMA* (It's That Man Again) with Tommy Handley and Dorothy Summers as Mrs Mopp.

SPIRIT -- TH BLITZ

ABOVE: Servicemen came home to a world much changed: familiar streets gone and a prefab for a home.

The Blitz spirit came to symbolize British resistance. Just as the heroic evacuation of troops from France by a flotilla of little ships in spring 1940 represented the 'Dunkirk spirit', so Britain's civilian population demonstrated equally dogged courage and resolve during sustained bombing in the winter of 1940–41.

The spirit of the Blitz was celebrated in film, poetry and in thousands of personal reminiscences. Almost every family in a blitzed town or city had its own stories of laughter mixed with tragedy: of people getting lost in the blackout, caught in the bath as the siren sounded, losing false teeth, rescuing buried pets, finding a car upended in the bomb crater outside. Others were left with permanent scars of loss: relatives, friends and neighbours who had become statistics, casualties of the bombing and destruction.

RIGHT: Revellers celebrate VE Day in 1945.

LEFT: Joyful victory crowds dancing in London.

RIGHT: Windmill Theatre dancers could put away their gas masks for good.

Social barriers relaxed. People felt they were 'all in it together'. They talked to strangers and gave them lifts, they slept on friends' couches after an evening out, they joked in endless queues.

Entertainers played their part. Members of ENSA (Entertainments National Service Association) gave concerts everywhere, from parish halls to Underground stations. The girls of London's Windmill Theatre earned their place in theatre history with the slogan 'We never close'.

The Blitz altered Britain's landscape. Coventry's old heart was gone, to be filled by a new kind of city centre in the 1950s. All over the great cities, holes gaped where once-familiar buildings had stood. Much of London's old East End and docklands disappeared. After the war, new high-density housing estates were built in neighbourhoods where people had once stood chatting at front doors or over the garden fence.

The Blitz passed into mythology. A famous cartoon of 1940 showed a soldier on the white cliffs of Dover with the words, 'Very well – alone!' During the Blitz, most Britons found they were not alone; bombs spared neither rank nor riches. The feeling that 'we're in this together' may have been temporary, but it contributed vastly to the national mood of resistance that ultimately led to final victory.

PLACES TO VISIT

The following is only a selection of places to visit about the Blitz. Many city museums have excellent exhibitions displaying what life was like locally during the Second World War.

Battle of Britain Memorial Flight, Coningsby, Lincolnshire
Tel: 01522 782040
www.raf.mod.uk/bbmf/bbmfhome.html
A guided tour of the hangar allows you to see a variety of still-operating aircraft, including a Lancaster, Spitfires and Hurricanes.

Bletchley Park, Milton Keynes, Bucks
Tel: 01908 640404 www.bletchleypark.org.uk
Find out about the pioneers who broke the 'Enigma' code and visit the Churchill Collection. The Blitz is remembered annually, with a fair and a brilliant display of fireworks.

ABOVE: Cabinet War Rooms.

Churchill Museum and Cabinet War Rooms, London Tel: 020 7930 6961 www.iwm.org.uk
These fortified basement rooms in Whitehall provided a safe place for Churchill and his advisors to make strategic decisions during the war. See the Transatlantic Telephone Room, the original 'hot-line' to the American president. The new Churchill Museum portrays the man he really was.

ABOVE: Chartwell, the home of Winston Churchill.

Chartwell, Westerham, Kent
Tel: 01732 866368 www.nationaltrust.org.uk
Churchill's home from 1924 until his death. Many of his possessions are on display, conveying the person-

ABOVE: Coventry's new cathedral stands beside the remnant of the medieval building destroyed in 1940, as a memory of the past and a hope for the future.

Winston Churchill's Britain at War Museum, London
Tel: 020 7403 3171 www.britainatwar.co.uk
Sounds, smells, even dust and smoke, take you right into the Blitz. A cinema broadcasts wartime news, and you can see what it was like sheltering in the London Underground.

Coventry Cathedral
Tel: 02476 267070 www.coventrycathedral.org.uk
Walk through the old cathedral ruins, a focus for prayer and reconciliation, into the splendour of the new cathedral.

Dover Castle, Kent
Tel: 0870 333 1181 www.english-heritage.org .uk
Visit the Secret Wartime Tunnels, Britain's only underground barracks, which include Churchill's Command Centre.

IWM Duxford, Cambridgeshire
Tel: 01223 835000 www.iwm.org.uk
Nearly 200 historic aircraft, together with tanks and military vehicles, can be seen. The many exhibitions include ones on the Battle of Britain and the Blitz. Items on display include an Anderson shelter you can look inside, and a V1 rocket ('Doodlebug').

ABOVE: Underground Command Centre,

Eden Camp, Malton, North Yorkshire
Tel: 01653 697777 www.edencamp.co.uk
This former prisoner-of-war camp consists of over 30 huts each displaying a different aspect of the Second World War. You can experience the sights, sounds and smells of a bomb attack in the Blitz.

The Guards Chapel, Wellington Barracks, London
Tel: 020 7414 3428 www.guards-shop.com/chapel
Tour the ruins of the chapel that a V2 rocket – watched by Churchill from Whitehall – destroyed.

HMS *Belfast*, London
Tel: 020 7940 6300 www.iwm.org.uk
This famous cruiser, moored in the Thames by Tower Bridge, served throughout the Second World War including the Normandy landings.

Imperial War Museum, London
Tel: 020 7416 5000 www.iwm.org.uk
Dedicated to all aspects of warfare, including 'The Blitz Experience', with a reconstruction of a bombed street and an air raid shelter showing what it was like being caught in an air attack.

Imperial War Museum North, Manchester
Tel: 0161 836 4000 www.iwm.org.uk
Take a look at the fire-fighting trailer pump used to put out the flames in the Manchester Blitz.

Kent Battle of Britain Museum, Folkestone, Kent
Tel: 01303 893140 www.kbobm.org
Visit the country's largest collection of Battle of Britain memorabilia.

National Army Museum, Chelsea, London
Tel: 020 7730 0717
www.national-army-museum.ac.uk
Find out all about the history of the army and a